In the Blink of an Eye

In the Blink of an Eye

Published by The Conrad Press in the United Kingdom 2022

Tel: +44(0)1227 472 874
www.theconradpress.com
info@theconradpress.com

ISBN 978-1-915494-21-4

Copyright © John Price, 2022

All rights reserved.

Typesetting and Cover Design by: Charlotte Mouncey, www.bookstyle.co.uk
The Conrad Press logo was designed by Maria Priestley.

Printed and bound in Great Britain by Clays Ltd, Elcograf S.p.A.

In the Blink of an Eye

John Price

Contents

Preface
In the blink of an eye   8

Morning
Childhood dreams   13
Memories of a little girl of ten   15
The man   17
Youth   19

A time to be living
The sea   22
The ghetto   23
My 'ouse   26
The good deed   28
The holiday   30

And a time to be loving
Ode to God   35
Moonlight   37
The lovers   39

A time to be parting
The lost dream   43
Parting   44
The last kiss   45

My rose	46
Autumn	47
The girl	48

A time to be thinking

Destiny???	50
Tears of clowns	51
The ballad of Patrick O'Sullivan	53
Kindness	55

And a time to be crying

Darkness	59
The old lady	60
The briefcase	61
James	62
The soldiers	63

A time to be silly

The doctor	69
Oddities	70
Stupidity	71
The bumblebee	72

Evening

The meeting	75
Dying embers	76
The old man	77

Epilogue

The rivers of time	80

Preface

In the blink of an eye

Yes, I was once here,
but I was gone in the blink of an eye.
You won't have noticed me,
because it was a short stay.

Yes, I was once here,
Few knew of my existence.
Apart from my wives, children, and friends,
no one remembered me.

Now they no longer exist,
and are now forgotten.
Yet they were once here,
but were gone in the blink of an eye.

Yes, I was once here,
as were millions before me.
But as is human destiny,
I was gone in the blink of an eye.

Yes, I was once here,
and reading these verses.
Perhaps you may think of me,
because, I was once here, and I did exist.

Yes, I was once here,
but I am now forgotten in the mists of time.
Yes I was once here,
but now no one remembers, or cares.

Morning

This first poem was written because I think that children today unfortunately seem to grow up far too quickly, and take everything for granted. I well remember the excitement of Christmas, birthdays, Guy Fawkes night (saving up to buy, and letting off, fireworks) and Easter when we had chicken eggs that mum and dad had drawn on.

They obviously couldn't afford chocolate eggs. Later generations have been spoilt. However, the dreams of my childhood live on, and that is the name of my first poem.

Childhood dreams

Sleep well my child,
and dream if you will.
Of giants and castles,
just over the hill.

Of witches on broomsticks,
and fairies and gnomes.
Of goblins and pixies,
and gingerbread homes.

Of animals dancing,
and dressing up smart.
Of treasure and pirates,
and an old faded chart.

Of magicians and wizards,
and vanishing cats.
Of toadies and piggies,
and belfries of bats.

Of princesses and princes,
and a palace of gold.
Of monsters and dragons,
and knights that were bold.

Sleep well sweet child,
as time surely will steal.
The dreams of your childhood,
When cares become real.

My next poem is probably the saddest, and certainly the most hard-hitting reflection on death that I have written. For this, I make no apologies.

The poem was written after I saw pictures of coffins of children, following bombings in Northern Ireland in the 1970's. This was bad enough. But how would I feel if I was the father of one of those children?

Memories of a little girl of ten

All I now have left, are my memories,
memories of a giggling little girl of ten.
Killed in a cause she knew nothing about,
shot dead in a crossfire of hatred.
Clutching a teddy bear.

She doesn't now hear the sound of the guns,
she won't ever know of the bitterness.
Of the cancerous hatred of bigots,
Of the evil of men.
Of her executioners.

So all I now have left are my memories,
of empty bedroom where she once slept.
A little girl saying her prayers,
In front of the fire.
Cuddling a teddy bear.

Memories of a small warm hand, tightly held,
a happy little girl with plaits,
A faded photograph,
A tattered schoolbook.
A bloodstained teddy bear.

She now sleeps under a white sheet of daisies,
still clutching her teddy bear,
and all that's left of a little girl of ten.
Is an inscription on a tombstone.
And my memories.

The next poem is dedicated to someone I knew extremely well. As a child she was unfortunately left at home every night when her parents went to the pub.

The poem attempts to express the horrors that she must have experienced, although it is inaccurate insofar that she had an adopted father.

The man

I live in a flat with my baby brother,
we haven't a dad, only a mother,
Each night she goes out and we're left on our own,
and we're so scared of being alone.

She kisses us both and turns off the light,
leaving us huddled together alone in the night,
We cower under the table our muscles all numb,
wondering whether the man will come.

My brother's asleep and I'm so full of fright,
please God, will you guard us tonight?
Make me brave, and keep us alive,
because I think the man will arrive.

I sit all night on the kitchen floor,
shaking in terror and watching the door.
Arm round my brother, clutching him tight,
as I'm sure that the man will come tonight.

Our little dog lies loyal by our side,
we tremble together, our fear we can't hide,
Someone's outside the door, perhaps it's our mum,
IT'S NOT, IT'S NOT! THE MAN HAS COME!

The door handle turns and I close my eyes,
my brother wakes up, and sits ups and cries.
My hearts stops beating, and we both lie down flat,
there's a horrible man is on the door mat

He's come to get us, of that I've no doubt,
I'm trembling all over as my Mum is still out.
He's going to kill us, I'm frantic with fear,
I scream, 'MUMMY! MUMMY! THE MAN IS HERE'.

We lie crying and sobbing under the table,
our dog would guard us if he was able,
He's whimpering and shaking, and nestles up near us,
but the man is hiding where we can't see.

The door opens, IT'S OUR MUM! ITS OUR MUM!
I know now tonight that the man won't come,
she enters the hall and turns on the light,
and we're safe from the man until tomorrow night.

The following poem is a somewhat flippant parody. However, I think that it has some merit, and therefore is worth including in this anthology of poems.

Youth

Youth, its elders does resent,
with biting words of dissent.
Ban it! Stop it! Don't conform!
They want to take the world by storm.
Why all this continual fuss?
It's a pity they can't be more like us.

A time to be living

My next poem I am quite proud of. It's called 'The sea'.

I like to think that it reflects the tides. Leave it to you to agree or not.

The sea

Water cold and crystal clear,
sea for evermore austere.
Salty element, gentle waves,
sinking boats and watery graves.
Water splashing wrinkled sand,
mysteries we don't understand.
Dancing horses, oceans free,
Untamed, strange, tempestuous sea.

My next poem while coming under the title of 'a time to be living,' should more correctly be entitled 'a time to exist.'

The ghetto

I know a place that God forgot,
where people live who matter not,
Where life meets death, without a care,
and children have no shoes to wear.

Where drunkenness and death are rife,
and people lowest form of life.
With filthy clothes and lice-filled hair,
and children have no shoes to wear.

The children roam around the street,
just sorting dustbins for things to eat.
At shops they only stop and stare,
they who have no shoes to wear.

Brutal men and gin-soaked wives,
frightened children, violent lives.
Callous acts and mortal fear,
where no one dares to shed a tear.

Life and death they matter not,
dead tramps lay, their bodies rot.
Sick people lay, no one to care,
starving babies with bodies bare.

Pregnant woman, with peroxide hair,
her open bed for men to share.
With dirty clothes, black stained sheet,
and unruly bastards around her feet.

Vicious dogs and starving cats,
no food to eat but mice and rats,
Where men get drunk and women swear,
but children have no shoes to wear.

No future can there ever be,
men and women cannot be free,
How long they live, who can tell,
before they leave their living hell.

I know a place that God forgot,
Where people live who matter not.
Where life meets death without a care,
and the children have no shoes to wear.

I think that it is about time that we had something a little bit more light hearted. 'So 'ere we go' with a poem entitled 'My 'ouse.' It is meant to be irony in the extreme, I hope that you agree!

My 'ouse

They've gone and knocked my 'ouse down,
and built a motorway,
In the cause of progress,
or so they always say.

It wasn't much to look at,
but was always 'ome to us,
Even when the rent went up,
we never made no fuss.

The 'ole street is in ruins,
as is 'alf the town.
They got a great big 'ammer,
and knocked my memories down.

What would my old mum say,
if she saw it now?
Our old 'ouse knocked to pieces,
by Christ! There'd be a row.

I thought I'd see the old town,
and went the other day,
The pub is standing all alone,
but the rest is motorway.

> My poor old 'ouse is gone,
> cars are 'ere to stay,
> The rat-infested 'ole is gone,
> a bleeding good job, I'd say.

My next poem was inspired by Betty (my aunt), who was asked by a vicar if she would attend the funeral of an old lady. The old lady had sadly died leaving no relatives or friends. My aunt went to the funeral, and found herself to be the only person present, apart from the vicar.

This was truly, a very tragic state of affairs, and ordinarily, would be too sad a subject on which I could write a poem. However, I decided that I could handle it; albeit in a humorous way. I therefore wrote this poem which is entitled, very appropriately, 'The good deed'.

The good deed

This 'ere vicar went and stopped me,
just the other day,
'E' arst me if I'd help 'im out,'
wiv a bint who'd passed away.

'Wot are you doin' Saturday?'
'E' arst quite casually,'
'I'd like your 'elp' to send 'er' off,'
but only if yer free.

It seems no one knew who she was,
or what she was and when,
And why she was or how she was,
or where she 'ad been then.

So I thinks about wot 'E' said,
and feelin' sort of kind,
I adn't got much on that day,
so I said I didn't mind.

The funeral was a queer 'un,'
and was a sight to see.
Wiv vicar standin' prayin',
surrounded by just me.

> 'E says, 'I don't know where she's bin,
> or where she oughta go,'
> Which sounded 'bloody funny,'
> for a vicar ought to know.
>
> But if she went to 'eaven,'
> and God 'arst' who saw 'er off,'
> She'd smile and say, 'I dunno,
> but 'E' were N'arfa Toff.'

My next poem is interesting insofar it has religious connotations. It reflects God's concern about his son being apparently tired and under the weather.

He (God) decides to send him (Jesus) on a holiday to improve his health. Whether God would choose to send his son on a holiday to Blackpool, rather than more exotic and sunny places such as Spain, is very debatable.

However, this poem indicates that he did choose Blackpool for all its faults.

The holiday

One day, up there up in heaven,
God saith unto his son.
You've been working too hard,
You're looking pale and wan.

You shall have a holiday,
but leave it up to me,
I'll go and make arrangements,
for Blackpool by the sea.

No sooner was it said,
than God exercised his power.
And Jesus was in Blackpool,
looking at the tower.

First he had some fish and chips,
and drank a pot of tea.
He ate a plate of whelks,
then paddled in the sea.

He sunbathed on the pier,
but at the end of the day.
Was feeling rather weary,
and sought a room to stay,

He tramped round in despair,
for every room was booked.
Inns, hotels, and boarding houses,
not one he overlooked.

Until at last, as time had past,
and it was late at night.
He met with a landlady
and related his sad plight.

Scornfully she stared at him,
then gave him the news.
'I would very much like to help you out,
but my husband doesn't like Jews.'

Then Jesus said, 'I understand
For there was no room at the inn,
I came to earth to save mankind
And save the world from sin.'

'My love is everlasting,'
He told the landlord's wife,
'All mankind is precious,
For that I gave my life.'

And a time to be loving

This poem concerns people's apparent love affair with their cars. It seems to me that this amounts to god worship, in other words, religion.

I do think that this is a mainly a man thing, however, women may be equally guilty. I could be wrong. Anyway, enjoy reading the poem.

Ode to God

Metallic God, shining bright,
heaven only knows your might.
Standing in your garage shrine,
O' great majestic car of mine.

On consecrated ground I stand,
with metal spanner in my hand.
Your precious body I do repair,
hurt by my unfair wear and tear.

At your crossply feet I kneel,
adjusting brakes and checking wheel.
Tyres and water, oil all right,
battery charged up every night.

Sundays are for family prayer,
to gleaming idol standing there.
Washing, cleaning, spit and polish,
for all our sins you thus abolish.

Us mortals dread and fear the day,
when you 'O Great One,' go away.
Your sacred parts they will derange,
and for better God will part exchange.

The following poem is pure indulgent romance, and probably unrealistic, and as such is totally over the top. However, some of us do have high spots in our lives, even if they don't last for very long. But they are good while they last. I pity those people who don't have those high spots.

So what? and why not? Anyway, as a reader of this poem you are stuck with this romance bit, so again, tough!

Moonlight

Bright moonlight shining down on me,
   casting bold reflections on the sea.
As I stand here in your heavenly rays,
   loving notions your love betrays.

While you hung suspended in the sky,
   people came to love in days gone by.
Folk alas! who have long since gone,
passed the night as you brightly shone.

Bygone lovers have shared each night,
   the thrill of love in your gentle light,
When night advanced and people slept,
   your romantic secrets were ever kept.

We can't tell what lies in store,
   but luminous ball shine evermore.
For romances past and those to be,
heavenly moon we give thanks to thee.

This next poem is a bit silly and is perhaps lightweight, however it does have an element of satire, and therefore is probably worth inclusion in this anthology.

The lovers

Where go you, my dears,
on this summers day.
With love in your hearts,
honest eyes does betray.

My dears you are really,
a handsomely pair,
A man of such valour,
and a lady so fair.

Your love is so true,
my dears, I detect,
So blissfully happy,
in every respect.

Old lady, Old lady,
how wrong is your source,
For we're going to court,
to get a divorce.

A time to be parting

This cluster of poems are about love lost. Again, I make no apologies. I think that we have all been there, and got the 'T' shirt. If we haven't, we probably haven't lived life to any extent, and can rightly be accused of being anoraks.

The lost dream

I sleep, by chance to dream of you,
of times gone by when love was true.
Of sunny days and dew-clad hills,
of fields of golden daffodils.

Of arms entwined in each embrace,
clinging tightly, and pulses race.
Of precious thoughts, and minds that touch,
Of words and dreams that matter much.

Of buttercups and fresh mown grass,
of magic moments with time to pass.
Of roses and the songs of birds,
of contented hearts, and endearing words.

Of April showers, and full bright moon,
or should I lie conscious, lest I wake too soon.
Summer is over, it's Autumn at last,
emptiness nears and my moment is past.

Parting

Should thou deem that love be put asunder,
that cherished bygone dreams should be discarded.
To be lost forever in the eternity of ages,
as but a far-off memory, to be regarded.

What then, if these things come to pass?
and over new pastures the future sun will set,
Life must surely be enriched by past love shared,
moments shared together, coveted without regret.

I forbid that thou should grieve upon the past,
but if thou will; tortured souls must part.
Then I shall go to my grave with the knowledge true,
that your name shall ever be remembered in my heart.

The last kiss

Before I sleep to dream no more,
just one last kiss my love,
A final lingering thought of thee,
before my soul be free.

So give me one last kiss my love,
as unknown darkness nears,
And a lonely soul sustain.
until we meet again.

My rose

Last night I lay in bed,
and drifted into sleep,
I dreamt I saw a rose,
that was mine alone to keep.

It's bloom was bright and perfect,
It's beauty clear to see,
For just a while, I held the rose,
until the sharp thorns scratched me.

For such a prize was not to be,
though I do beseech,
The rose will not forever be,
always out of reach.

Autumn

Trees have shed their leaves,
and look so naked and bare.
Autumn leaves of reddish brown,
lie dying everywhere.

Summer is but a memory,
the things that we did are past,
The happy times we had, that,
we knew could never last.

The sun has lost its warmth,
soon winter will appear,
Time for a parting kiss,
before the frost is here.

The skies a watery blue,
it's so cold now you have gone,
But I think of the warmth of summer,
and your sweet memory lingers on.

The girl

There was a girl
who was so fair,
of classic beauty
and long blonde hair.
Men loved her, but
her heart was cold,
So she lived alone
when she was old.

A time to be thinking

Destiny???

It is the twilight of man's folly,
as the dark clouds gather in the sky.
Just like a shroud,
A black shroud,
Impatient for the world to die.

The end of mankind is at hand,
as the evil vultures of hell.
Wait for the kill,
the final kill.
And for Satan to ring the bell.

The very last rights have been spoken,
and man granted his last request.
Death by suicide,
by suicide.
And the human race, laid to rest.

Tears of clowns

Why is it when we cry we laugh,
and when we laugh we cry,
can't always tell the difference,,,
however hard we try?

Our lives are unpredictable,
with all their ups and downs,
and happiness we feel today.
Can drown in tears of clowns.

Tears and laughter mingle,
about ourselves we learn.
So let the wheel of fortune,
Spin round another turn.

Concrete jungle

Concrete jungle of unrest,
overcrowded hornets nest,
Metal girders, sheets of glass,
tiny square of trampled grass.

Rabbit hutches, high rise blocks,
washing lines with dripping frocks,
Parents out at work all day,
children left alone to play.

Old folk with no will to manage,
gangs of youths, causing damage,
Families each in separate cells,
suffer in their concrete hells.

The ballad of Patrick O'Sullivan

Patrick O'Sullivan came over from Eire,
wild he was with bright red hair.
Wherever he went he wanted to fight,
and he came home battle-scarred every night.

He drank so much it made folk concerned,
and the time to stop he never learned,
He boozed and scrapped, and boozed some more,
and many a time got caught by the law.

But Patrick wasn't completely bad,
because a better side he no doubt had.
He made it right, or more or less,
For each Sunday to the Father he did confess.

Then one dark night he picked a fight,
with a navvy from a building site,
The man was drunk with reason diminished,
he lunged with a knife and poor Patrick was finished.

Patrick fell dying, stabbed through the heart,
His wild eyes ablaze as this life did depart.
He lay there so still, such a terrible sight,
That folk still remember that tragic night.

His coffin was covered all over with green,
A finer sight as ever was seen.
The pubs closed early all over the town,
The drunks were all there to see Patrick put down.

Everyone went, the sadness to share,
The Father spoke up with a comforting prayer,
'His life was not wasted, for deny if you can,
for here lies the remains of a God-fearing man.'

Kindness

Kindness soothes an anxious breast
and feeds a lonely heart.
Gives respite to our deepest fears
when long loved ones depart.
Kindness is as kindness does
with love it's counterpart,
No greater joy can ever be,
Than the kindness we impart.

And a time to be crying

The following poems are about things that none of us want to think about. They concern hard hitting issues which we generally try to avoid even thinking about. You have started to read this anthology of poems, and I beg you to finish, whether it upsets you or not.

The first poem is entitled 'Darkness' and is about a blind boy shunned and ignored by the world. 'The old lady' follows which gives insights into our own destinies. 'The briefcase' is about a pub bombing. 'James' is about a forlorn soldier. 'The Soldiers' is a tragic and pathetic conclusion which does no credit to us as a race of people.

The group of poems is entitled 'And a time to be crying.'

Darkness

It's shameful that the boy is blind,
always a burden on mankind.
Poor wretch, he never made the choice,
of only hearing mother's voice.

See him groping in the dark,
ignored by the other kids, in the park.
Mother alone, sees no disgrace,
In the son, who'll never see her face.

The old lady

I looked into the old lady's face,
and I saw the strain left,
Of three score years and ten of life on this earth,
of the struggles and battles.
That were won and lost.

The triumphs over disaster, achieved,
just merely to exist.
I asked myself,
'For what purpose?'
What is the reason for existing?

Perhaps there is a reason,
not yet shown to me.
When I looked into her face,
I saw tiredness and resignation,
and acceptance of her fate.

But perhaps, worst of all,
I thought I saw myself,
In the years to come.

The briefcase

The bar was crowded with people,
a harmless crowd without doubt.
Ordinary men and women,
Just enjoying a pleasant night out.

The stranger came in very quietly,
not a soul knew he was there,
He put a briefcase against the bar,
and stood in the background to stare.

The pub was then blown into pieces,
five men died instantly there,
The stench of spilt blood was strong,
and black smoke polluted the air.

The terrorist stood grimly smiling,
whilst people were openly crying,
The injured were taken away,
with the dead, and the wounded, and dying.

We can boast of our civilisation.
but how do we take on the chore,
Of telling the victims' poor children,
that they won't see their parents no more.

James

James was a brave and young soldier,
who got bolder as he got older.
He would not retreat,
or sit on his seat ,
So now he's not bolder but colder.

The soldiers

Could one single tear be shed,
for all our soldiers,
long since dead.

Who died to make a better place,
and give some future, to our race.
But sacrifice was all in vain, for men went back,
to war again.

Now graves lie lonely and obscure,
and why men died,
we're now unsure.

Our thanks to them was overdue,
as on their graves,
the long grass grew.

But let our grateful prayers be said,
For all our soldiers,
long since dead.

Lonesome

Lonesome is the man,
Who does fame and fortune seek,
who turns his back on plainness,
and all that's just and meek,
for him the world is barren,
with no place to rest his head,
a world without a meaning,
until he ere be dead.

Lonesome is that man,
who is doomed to grief and pain,
by travelling that lonesome path,
for greed and selfish gain.
For his is just an empty soul,
just waiting for the touch,
of the milk of human comfort,
that means so very much.

Lonesome is the man,
who enquires not of others health,
who abandons truth and charity,
for the sake of worldly wealth,
for man can never live alone,
in solitary confinement,
Life has to have a reason,
and meek, humane, refinement.

A time to be silly

This next set of poems are silly, I make no apologies for this as they perhaps make up for the very serious issues addressed by my earlier poems. 'The doctor' is I think quite witty, 'Oddities' is perhaps a little more perceptive, as is 'Stupidity.' Finally, there is 'The bumble bee' for which I have provided a separate introduction.

The doctor

Mr Quack, the doctor,
had a splendid notion,
To ensure perpetual life,
by a simple potion.

He drank the potion in a gulp,
then followed a commotion,
He hadn't found his long-lost youth,
but just perpetual motion.

Oddities

I like ice cream,
and I like jelly.
Kicking dogs,
and watching telly.

I'm the greatest,
and so good.
I'm the best,
and thick as wood.

Stupidity

'Where have you been?'
God said out aloud.
'You weren't at the gates.
Or home in your cloud.'

'I'm sorry,' said Peter.
'I've been for a rest.
Works been so hectic,
I'm doing my best.'

'Men are so stupid.
As you know my brother.
They keep having wars,
and killing each other.'

Finally, this is probably the most silly poem that I have ever written. Hopefully, in its own humble way, it emulates the style of the great Lewis Carroll. The poem is entitled 'The bumble bee.'

The bumblebee

The humble slee sat bilently,
in the baggage snatch,
As the flutter sly went gloating by.
across the baggage snatch.

The humble slee, huzzed mangrily,
in the baggage snatch,
As the flutter sly went gloating by,
He sprainly houldn't smatch.

The flutter sly huzzed mangrily,
in the baggage smatch,
As the flutter sly, went gloating by,
across the baggage smatch.

Evening

These last three poems, I must rank amongst the best that I have written. They each deal with old age and death. The first poem, 'The meeting,' deals with these subjects in a very light hearted way. The poem suggests that our possible appearance in heaven will somehow be based on a lottery of the virtues that we have shown in life, (I doubt it,) but a lot of people do believe it to be true.

The final two poems approach the subject of old age and death far more seriously. The second poem is entitled 'Dying embers,' and is particularly hard hitting. Hopefully it makes us all look at ourselves. Maybe it will make us feel guilty about our failures to care about the elderly, and to do something to help them.

The third poem in this section is called 'The old man.' I have no doubt in my mind, that this is the most poignant poem that I have written. It concerns the last moments of an old man's life. I do believe that this it is the best poem that I have written. I also think that it is the poem that I would most wish to be remembered by.

The meeting

Three old men by chance did meet,
and sat and talked upon a seat.
The first thought hard, and then he said,
'I'm satisfied with the life I've led.

'I've been a good man all my life,
and always been faithful to my wife,
For when death comes, heaven I'll see,
God warmly welcomes the likes of me.'

The second man then thought aloud,
'Of my good life I'm also proud,
I've never smoked or lived in sin,
A place in heaven I'm sure to win.'

The third man then thought for a while,
and then related with a smile.
'I've not been good, I must confess,
In fact life's been an utter mess.

'I've boozed and gambled all my life,
Rarely been faithful to my wife.
I've not been good but downright bad,
You want to know? I'm bloody glad.'

Dying embers

Huddled in front of the fire,
is the little old lady of grey.
Rubbing gnarled hands, to keep warm,
at the end of another cold day.

Forgotten by a world with no time,
hunger and need be her fate.
Red tearful eyes keep a watch,
as the embers die in the grate.

The old man

Old man sitting all alone,
looking at the sky.
and thinking of the past,
wipes tear from bloodshot eye.

Old man thinks of loving wife,
and the day that he was wed.
Of the gentle loving touch,
of a wife now long since dead.

Old man feeling very tired,
lifts his weary head.
struggles up on withered legs,
and shuffles off to bed.

Old man lays between the sheets,
just looking at the ceiling.
Body riddled with disease,
and muscles void of feeling.

Old man now is dreaming,
of what life might have been.
Death draws ever nearer,
with perils quite unseen.

Old man laying very still,
blood has stopped its flow.
Fate has intervened.
and struck its final blow.

Epilogue

The rivers of time

The rivers of time,
run down to the sea.
Twisting and turning,
like a wild apple tree.

Now is the evening,
and so let it be.
As life runs out,
for you and for me.

THE END